What the Gratitude List
Said to the Bucket List

What the Gratitude List
Said to the Bucket List

by

Gloria Heffernan

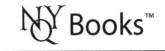

The New York Quarterly Foundation, Inc.
Beacon, New York

NYQ Books™ is an imprint of The New York Quarterly Foundation, Inc.

The New York Quarterly Foundation, Inc.
P. O. Box 470
Beacon, NY 12508

www.nyq.org

First Edition

Set in New Baskerville

Layout by Raymond P. Hammond

Cover Design by Rachel Ablan

Cover Photograph by Dan Roche

Author Photo by Jim Heffernan

Library of Congress Control Number: 2019947953

ISBN: 978-1-63045-067-0

For My Great-Nephews
Daniel and Brayden Beers

These poems have appeared or will appear in the following journals:

"Some of Our Parts," *CNY Branch of American Pen Women/ Syracuse Post Standard*
"Rotunda," *Folio*
"She Weeps for Camelot," *Evening Street Review*
"Sailing," *Southword*
"Astronomy," *Jabberwock Review*
"The Girls of Paris," *The Columbia Review*
"Taking Her Vitals," *Blood and Thunder*
"My Sister's Glasses," *The Healing Muse*
"Kaddish for My Sister," *Evening Street Review*
"Sniper Fire," *Evening Street Review*
"Reading a Life," *Naugatuck River Review*
"A Greening of Sorts," *The Healing Muse*
"Pearl," *Narrative Northeast*
"Shrapnel," *Burningwood Literary Journal*
"Insomnia," *Gargoyle*
"Field Notes," *Tipton Poetry Review**
"Let Morning Come," *The Healing Muse*
"The Family We Choose," *Louisville Review*
"What the Gratitude List Said to the Bucket List," *Mason's Road Literary Journal*
"Mass of Remembrance," *Anchor Magazine*
"Love Letter to Tomorrow," *Cold Noon*
"Hiking Koko," *The Healing Muse*
"Rescue at Koko Crater," *Snapdragon: A Journal of Healing and Art*
"Paradise Found," *Badlands Literary Review*
"The Gardens at the Villa Lecchi," *Cold Noon*
"At the Gutenberg Museum," *Worcester Review*
"Red Carpet," *Blood and Thunder*
"Praise Song for the Hospice Nurse," *Chautauqua Literary Journal*
"Ten Rings," *Stone Canoe*
"The Green Room," *Parody*
"The Prodigal's Sister," *Evening Street Review*
"Souvenir," *The Comstock Review*

"Snowy Egret—Avery Island, Louisiana," *Grey Sparrow Journal*
"The Wild Boars of Fukushima," *Awake in the World,* vol. 2.,
        Riverfeet Press
"Celtic Wind," *Icarus*
"Watching Billy Collins Read His Poems," *Two Words For*
"Dear Mary Oliver," *The Wayfarer: A Journal of Contemplative
        Literature*
"Submission," *Emrys Journal*

*The following poems appeared in my chapbook, Some of Our Parts,
from Finishing Line Press:*

"Some of Our Parts"
"She Weeps for Camelot"
"The Girls of Paris"
"All Through the Night"
"Double Exposure"
"Evening in Paris"
"Scent Memory"
"Cursive"
"Taking Her Vitals"
"My Sister's Glasses"
"Kaddish for My Sister"
"Let Morning Come"
"The Family We Choose"
"What I Want"
"Wisdom Quilt"

Contents

What the Gratitude List Said to the Bucket List

Some of Our Parts

I believe in Frida Kahlo's moustache,
Eleanor Roosevelt's buck teeth,
Maya Angelou's wrinkled forehead.

I believe in the small round wart
nested in the crease between my mother's
nose and left cheek,
I believe in my sister's thinning hair,
my best friend's gapped teeth,
my stretch marks and thick waist.

I believe that some of our parts
are no match for the sum of our parts
and I believe the sum of our parts
is holy indeed.

Rotunda

I.
The black and white television
plays ceaselessly for days.
I fall asleep to sorrowful voices
pouring down the hall to my bed,
learning the vocabulary of grief.

My mother stops to listen
between loads of laundry
all the while telling me she is fine,
just as she did after my father's funeral
when I was presumably
too young to mourn.

I wonder if there will ever
be anything else on television
as I try to fit together the puzzle pieces
of strange new words—
lying in state,
eternal flame,
assassination.

A black ribbon of mourners
ten miles long
lines the streets outside the Capitol,
oblivious to November chill,
waiting to file past the casket,
and pay their respects to the first
President I know by name.

II.
The newsman
in a reverent tone
describes the muffled footsteps
moving in a measured pace
over the marbled floor
of the *Rotunda*.

The word finds its way
into my mouth
like a piece of ripe fruit.

Rotunda.
I roll its round edges
over my four-year-old tongue,
and feel the *t* and the *d*
tapping the roof of my mouth
like a blind man's cane.

He repeats it,
day after day,
drawing me deeper into
the maze of language,
mesmerizing me with its
texture and taste,
and while the nation grieves,
I fall in love
with the mystery of words.

She Weeps for Camelot

Stepping out in front of his mother,
he raises his hand in salute,
already so poised
before the cameras.
It is his birthday today.
He is three years old,
Camelot's youngest prince
bidding his father farewell.

My mother watches weeping.
Her three-year-old son sleeps
on the couch by her side
as she remembers the funeral
ten months earlier
when the wind whipped
the veil that covered her face
as they handed her the tri-fold flag.

The First Lady holds
her daughter's hand
as my mother holds mine.
Silence envelopes the nation
like the black veil that covers
the young widow's face.
Even the November wind is still
as she stares ahead, a study in dignity.

Jersey City is not Camelot,
And my mother no American royalty.
But watching the flag-draped casket
roll past the Cathedral steps
she sees only a widow and her children,
and grieves for a shattered family
as her three-year-old son
stirs in his sleep.

Sailing

A dead roach floats on the surface
of my mother's afternoon coffee.
She watches its compatriots
scale the wall above the stove
as if they know she cannot
douse them with Raid
while dinner is cooking.
She doesn't know if roaches laugh,
but she imagines they do on days like this
when all the scrubbing in the world

seems to be for naught.
She dumps the coffee down the drain
and wipes her hands
on the green housecoat she wears
to hang out the window
clipping freshly laundered sheets to the clothesline,
watching them snap and billow in the wind
like the graceful sails of a schooner
she wishes she could board with her children
and sail away to someplace clean.

Astronomy

Black hole,
sucking every planet
into its vortex,
reducing matter
to a single point,
extinguishing all light,
galactic undertow heaving
the entire cosmos
into its gullet.

She lies on the couch
in the dark,
flicks ashes
into her empty coffee cup.
The child stands in the doorway.
"Mommy, are you okay?"
"Fine," she replies,
stretching the single syllable
as far as it will go
like molten glass
before it becomes brittle
and breaks.

"Go back to bed."
The child lingers
but obeys,
a tiny asteroid
powerless against
the gravitational pull
of darkness.

The Girls of Paris

No matter their age,
they were always *the girls*,
dressed in starched white uniforms,
and white rubber soled shoes.
They might have been nurses
lined up at the bus stop after closing time,
if not for their black aprons
dusty with powdered sugar.

The girls have blisters on their feet,
running back and forth
behind the counter all day,
and blisters on their hands
breaking the red and white string
spooling from the ceiling
for the cardboard boxes
embossed with a gold Eiffel Tower.

"Take a number, please."
The line spills out the door
on Sunday mornings
when church bells ring over Jersey City,
and the girls brace themselves
for the wave of saints and sinners
descending on the bakery
after the final hymn is sung.

"Six apple turnovers,"
orders the lady in the blue felt hat.
"Gimme a pound cake, and a babka,"
bellows the man in the pinstriped suit,
snapping his pocket watch for effect.
"Birthday cake pick up—
No, it's Cathy with a C, dammit.
Can't you read?"

She flips the sign in the window
from Come-in-We're-Open
to Sorry-We're-Closed,
and scrapes the crumbs
from the heavy trays
to scrub for tomorrow's rush.

The girls get their pick of anything
left at the end of the day.
They stock up on cheese Danish
and apple crumb cake.
She picks up her box
tied with red and white string.
Butter cookies tonight.
The kids will be happy.

All Through the Night

Sleep, my child,
And peace attend thee...

The fan hums softly on the night table,
its quiet song muffles
Johnny Carson's monologue
in the next room
where my mother submits
to another sleepless night.
The soft electric breeze
pulls a plume of cigarette smoke
through the doorway,
scenting my room
with Salem 100's
and Jean Naté.

The gentle whir rescues me
from the silence
where my too vivid imagination
ponders the finer points of death.
But *where is* Daddy?
But *what is* heaven?
She doesn't know how to answer
a four-year old ruminating on mortality,
so offers as substitute
an amber-eyed Jesus
enthroned in ornate brass frame
complete with nightlight
and plastic roses.

Enveloped in the white noise,
Jesus watches from his perch
on the chest of drawers
while my mother kneels
beside me teaching me to pray.

If I die before I wake...
I stumble over the words,
race to the amen,
and practice holding my breath
to fool death if it should sneak
in through the fire escape.

The fan hums its tuneless melody
all through the night—
a lullaby of sorts
while I watch the shadows from the TV
flicker across the wall,
listen to the muffled laughter
and the blare of Doc's trumpet—
anything to resist the threat of slumber.

Double Exposure

Forty years later
they hold the framed photo
taken when they were four and five years old.
She in a blue jumper,
hair curled into stiff coils
after sleeping in pink foam rollers all night.
He in a blue polo shirt
pressed neatly for the occasion.
Their father's blue eyes blending with
their mother's pug nose.

The long-forgotten picture
reprinted and framed for each of them,
a Christmas gift from their mother's granddaughter
who insists they pose with it now,
a testament to enduring smiles
etched into faces resembling her own.
She positions them in a mirror image of the original,
her father on the left, her aunt on the right,
the children they were
still present in the middle-aged faces that fill the lens.
She urges them to smile

just as their mother urged them
when the Sears photographer
came to the tenement apartment,
setting up the lights and tripod
to capture the smiles
that proved they would be all right
even as they tried to understand
why their father's heart attacked him.

Now she frames the same image,
focuses on the same faces,
shoots as all say *"Cheese,"*
preserving the enduring smiles
that prove they will be all right,
even on this first Christmas
without her grandmother.

Evening in Paris

Her favorite shade of blue
a cobalt teardrop
crowned in pleated silver cap
evoking the Eiffel Tower
at midnight

Evening in Paris
born in 1928
just like my mother
awash in jasmine and bergamot
dabbed on each pulse point

She saves the empty bottles
to perfume her lingerie drawer
and scent the hankie
she carries in her purse
to wipe our dripping noses

Ninety-nine cents
at the Five and Ten
and me with a dollar
in my pocket
on Christmas Eve

The new bottle swaddled
in its satin lined box
centered on her dresser
next to the Jean Naté
and Jergens Lotion
waiting for a special occasion

Scent Memory

I thought that was just
what men smelled like,
Big Jack, Uncle Pete, Ray the super.
I didn't know it was a blend
of whiskey, beer, sweat, and Old Spice.
It was the smell of absence,
the smell of the empty space
once occupied by my father
who liked to stop at the White Owl Tavern
now and then
for a quick Boiler Maker
and a few laughs with the guys.

When Uncle Pete came by after dinner
neat in his blue uniform,
service revolver holstered at his waist,
my mother bit her lip
remembering her stepfather roaring
up the street singing "The Old Rugged Cross,"
a sure bet it would be a long night
laced with threats and taunting
with the gun he stored
in a box in the hall closet.

I didn't know that the pigeon-toed man
lurching into the kitchen
with a paper bag under one arm was drunk
as he swept Eddie and me
into a Pabst-Blue-Ribbon-hug.
He was just loud and funny,
squeezing into one of the child-sized rockers
my mother had bought on lay-away
that first Christmas after my father died.

Quietly watchful,
she extended a chilly hospitality
to her late husband's brother.
Eager to avoid a fight,
she gently corralled us
to the far corner of the kitchen,
while he held court from his pint-sized perch,
until she told him not to open the bag
when he demanded a glass.

His dark brows knit together.
"If that's the way you want it," he said,
listing to his full six feet
with the tiny wooden rocker
clinging to his rear end like a child
who refused to let go.

As he wriggled his hips,
Eddie and I pealed with laughter
unaware of the mounting tension
as he struggled to free himself
without falling face first
onto the black and white linoleum,
until he finally shoved the handles
and flung the chair to the floor.

She followed him to the door,
warning him never to return
with whiskey on his breath
and a gun at his hip.

Then she silently walked
back to the kitchen,
righted the rocking chair
and tried to silence
"The Old Rugged Cross"
echoing through her brain.

Cursive

Her right hand,
twice the size of mine,
envelopes my left.

Pencil sharpened
and vertical,
she leads the dance
across the sky blue
lines on the page.

First the *G*,
lines and loops,
uphill and down,
like the first bike ride
with training wheels.

Her hand steers mine.
Now the graceful
glide up into the
elegant oval of *l*.
Down again
for the squat round *o*.

My sister teaches me
to write my name.
After ten practice runs
with her strong hand
holding on to guide and balance,
she removes the training wheels
and pushes me off.

I grip the pencil,
pedal slowly, methodically.
There it is—
my hand, my name,
my sister launching me
onto the page.

29

Taking Her Vitals

I carry memories of the ICU
in the bottom of my purse
like a forgotten thumb tack
that pierces my finger
every time I reach in to find my keys.
It's always 2:00 a.m.
the night nurse taking her vitals
as if they were spare parts
to be carried away one at a time,
inexorably dismantling respiration
pulse, oxygen level, blood pressure,
urine output, Bilirubin count—
clinical words intersecting
in a crossword puzzle
where Across and Down hold clues
with no answers
and the medically-induced coma
robs us of her days.
No, she is not Bed 4,
she is my sister.
I dwell in the chrome-legged chair
with the yellow plastic seat
beside her bed
hypnotized by the rhythm
of machines that blink and beep and buzz,
taking her vitals as she sleeps.

Kaddish for My Sister

In Memory of Alicia Cahill Goldberg
July 22, 1949 – July 3, 2002

The seven days of mourning have passed.
We have walked around the block,
dismantled the shiva boxes,
taken the covers off the mirrors.

I look at my reflection,
searching for the image
so many have found there
—your face—

All I see now
are the swollen eyes and puffy cheeks
that bear witness to a week of tears
as my fingers drift automatically to the
gold cross at my throat,
a gift from you two Christmases ago.

All I see now
are the dirt and stones
raining down on your casket
as the Rabbi translates patiently,
letting me know when to say Amen.

All I see now
is a plate of glass reflecting a face
I hardly recognize.
I drop the sheet back over the mirror.
There is nothing there that I need to see.
The mirror I looked to all my life
is gone.

My Sister's Glasses

My sister's trifocals
are zipped into
a quilted pouch
in my top dresser drawer
between the silk scarves
and the pantyhose.

Glaucoma had
chewed at the edges of
her eyesight,
like a rat devouring
still living prey.
Encroaching darkness

never dimmed her light.
Just one more obstacle
in a lifetime of
obstacles overcome
or overlooked.

I have saved them
since that morning
over a decade ago
when I collected
her belongings
from the ICU,

as if they might
somehow be the lens
through which
I could see the world
once more
through her eyes.

Sniper Fire

Target acquired, the sniper rolls down the window.
Walking my dog, I never see it coming.
"Fat bitch," he screams as the car speeds away.

Shot fired through snarling teeth and twisted lips.
My reflexes too slow to avoid the impact.
Target acquired, the sniper rolls down the window.

Drunken laughter pours out the rear window
like the curl of smoke after a freshly discharged round.
"Fat bitch," he screams as the car speeds away.

Heads turn in the wake of the anonymous assailant.
Some snicker, some avert their eyes.
Target acquired, the sniper rolls down the window.

I reel as the dog waits to resume our walk.
Still recoiling from the blast I check for damage.
"Fat bitch," he screams as the car speeds away.

No blood, nothing to bind or bandage.
Just another flesh wound, after all.
Target acquired, the sniper rolls down the window.
"Fat bitch," he screams as the car speeds away.

Not Your Average Garage Sale

This is not just any garage sale.
The six-foot folding tables lining the driveway
are strewn with things too costly to price
so just make me an offer and we'll deal.

That coffee cup with the broken handle, for example.
It burned my lips when I poured out the words
that I can never take back.
But I've saved the pieces
and if you glue them back together
it will be good as new.

And just take a look at the table with all those mirrors.
Don't mind the cracks—
You won't get the seven years bad luck,
so you can gaze into them risk-free.
Don't be alarmed if the images
are somewhat distorted.
That's what mirrors are for, after all.

And then there's that answering machine over there—
It's old but it still works perfectly.
There's just that one message—
from the day before she committed suicide.
I know it's just a coincidence,
but I can't figure out how
to make that red light stop blinking.

Reading a Life

Mary Rose Kelly is dead.
She was a lover of Yeats and Agatha Christie,
Italian cooking, gardening and bird-watching.
Tucked into a hard-covered 1946 edition of Yeats's *The Rose,*
is a funeral card with a picture of the Sacred Heart of Jesus,
commemorating Edward Joseph Kelly,
1918-1963— her husband,
who died too young but lived long enough
to see an Irishman in the White House.

I never met Mary Rose Kelly—
not until today when I found
the 27 books in the Nearly New Shop
with her name printed impeccably
in the upper right-hand corner of every title page.
It was her daughter, I imagine,
who packed the books
and sorted them by author
and decided to leave the dust jackets on
even though some were tattered and discolored.

Maybe the forgotten prayer card
wasn't forgotten at all but instead
a way of telling whoever found the book
that she had loved her Eddie who inscribed it
"To my own Rose on our first anniversary."
Perhaps she had made a ritual
of revisiting it every year,
reciting aloud her favorites
as she obeyed the poet's instruction to
take down this book and slowly read.

I choose *The Rose,* priced at $2.00,
because I like the tired dust jacket
with the water ring where
Mary Rose must have once placed
a cup of tea when she ran to answer the phone
and probably moaned, *"Oh no,"*
when she found the stain later.
And then I take down the Reader's Digest edition
of Agatha Christie stories because,
just like Mary Rose,
I've always loved a good mystery.

A Greening of Sorts

It only appears to happen suddenly—
the voluptuous explosion of green leaves
painting the hillside
that April morning
when just a day earlier
the trees looked like
a child's stick figures.

But it wasn't one sudden lavish brush stroke.
The build-up was gradual—first a dull red bud
barely visible on the tip of the branch.
And then, the hull of the bud broke away
and underneath, a pale green kernel
ripened unnoticed for days.

And still it seemed the buds would never fill out
into something resembling a maple leaf,
until that morning when you
looked out the kitchen window
over the rim of your coffee cup
and there it was,
evidence that spring had kept its promise.

That's what it was like when the green and yellow capsule
finally made its presence known.
It only seemed sudden when I found myself speaking
without choking back tears,
when I could drive the car
without fearing a truck might be hidden in my blind spot,
when I could watch the news
without feeling I was swallowing poison.

A month or so of imperceptible progress,
a gradual balancing of serotonin,
a slow surrender to the reality
that depression is an illness—
not a character defect,
and in what seems like only a moment,
the grip of winter
loosens its hold on my throat.

Pearl

Iridescence born of irritation,
the traditional gift
marking thirty years of marriage.

"Never much cared for pearls,"
she says, taking a drag on the lipstick-
stained cigarette that smells
like tomorrow's dirty laundry.

They loved each other once,
before the grains of sand
got trapped in the nacre,
calcifying layer upon layer.

Nicotine and resentment
emanate from her pores,
like ribbons of steam
from a rusty kettle.

She taps the beads against her teeth,
testing their authenticity,
imagining the oysters
that produced them.

"I guess they're the real thing,"
she says, exhaling a long puff of smoke
and wondering what gems
today's irritants may yield.

Shrapnel

My words ricochet
back into my face,
splintering flesh
with the impact
of mindless syllables
muttered under my breath,
barely audible
but heard nonetheless.

Words spewed
into the atmosphere,
involuntary but vile,
words I should have vomited
into any empty vessel
and plugged with
a lead stopper.

Words spilled
onto sacred ground,
scattered in a garden
for the innocent
to find like tantalizing
red berries
on a poisonous bush.

Field Notes: Hand

Subject studied
in natural habitat:

It chops the onions
for tonight's chili.
Observe the way the fingers
curl around the knife handle
making smooth vertical cuts
that release the gases
that burn the eyes
and summon the tears.

Watch it clip the leash
to the dog's collar,
and coil the long strap
twice around the wrist
to keep a firm hold
in case he decides to chase
the neighbor's cat.

Study the way it handles
the steering wheel,
the subtle movements
that keep the car centered in the lane,
the easy flick of the index finger
turning the blinker on,
the smooth return to the wheel.

Observe it like a scientist
on a field expedition studying
the behavior of a moth—
so common a thing
until you try to count its wingbeats
or describe its flight pattern.

And then a meat cleaver
falls from the sky.

Don't ask me how
or where it came from.
Shit happens.
Just keep taking notes.

It drops with a thud
striking the subject
at a 90 degree angle
severing the hand
at the wrist.

No explanation.
No one to blame.
Just something that happens.
A variable to be observed.
The subject will learn to adjust.

She will find other ways
to chop an onion,
walk the dog,
drive from point A to point B.

She will learn to endure
the phantom pains
in nerve endings
that remember what
used to be there.
In time they will be
a welcome reminder
of how far she has come.

But that's a hypothesis
for another study.
For now, I must
type up these field notes.
It takes twice as long
with just one hand.

Let Morning Come

after Jane Kenyon's "Let Evening Come"

Let the darkness of the long night
recede from the city's rooftops, blending
morning with mourning as the sun rises.

Let the taxis barrel down the streets
as if there were somewhere to go beyond
this hospital room. Let morning come.

Let the unopened envelopes pile up
in the mailbox. Let sunlight pour into
your kitchen where dishes still litter the sink.

Let pictures in their frames recall happier days.
Let the neighbors wonder about the woman
taken away in an ambulance. Let mourning come.

To the milk carton in the refrigerator, to the blinking
light on the answering machine, to the ones
left behind, let morning come.

Let cold wind blow, as it will, and don't
be afraid. Grief is the outer fabric of a coat
lined with gratitude, so let mourning come.

The Family We Choose

Every room overflows with your presence—
a strand of pearls for my twenty-first birthday,
the Celtic Cross you embroidered for my fiftieth,
the tool box you gave me one Christmas,
filled with all I might ever need for home repair—
*"Because every woman should know how
to use a power drill."*

When the phone rings at 2:00 a.m.,
I know the calls you didn't return last night
were portents of more than a night on the town.
The doctor calls looking for next of kin.
After forty years, we are kin indeed.
"I suggest you come right away,"
she advises, clinical voice steeped in calm.

At eighteen, we dubbed ourselves
best friends.
Time made us sisters.
"We are the family we choose," you said
when we celebrated birthdays and mourned losses,
welcomed each new generation,
laughed and cried without a word.

Now in the ICU,
where I stroked your forehead
as you surrendered your last breath,
the machines have gone eerily quiet.
Lights on monitors that blinked
only moments ago are dark and still.
There is nothing left to fix.

The family we chose is shattered.
Your toolbox is suddenly empty
having finally faced the one thing
you could not repair—
not even with your safety goggles
and power drill.

Prayer of Lamentation and Remembrance

Lord, help me to recall her life
when the darkness of her death
threatens to engulf all memory.

Help me to remember her laughter,
loud and deep and full-bellied.
Let me recall her face in repose,
reading poetry or embroidering a pillow.

Help me to remember our first airplane ride
when we traveled to Ireland,
and her transcendent look as she studied
the illuminated pages of the Book of Kells.

Help me to remember her reckless generosity,
the gifts she chose with such care,
and gave with such joy,
even when the giving meant doing without.

Help me to remember her quiet presence,
her willingness to share the darkest moments,
never trying to erase the pain
but always willing to share it.

Help me to whisper a thousand thank you's
for the blessings of her friendship
when I need to quell the raging grief
that wants only to scream,
Too soon.

Tinnitus, 3:00 a.m.

Cicadas invade my middle ear—
a needle of sound
piercing the silence.

Their single high pitched note,
a tuneless keening

a shrieking tea kettle
whistling all night long.

No respite.
Just that single note,
rendering sleep
an impossible dream.

Insomnia

He worries that his snoring bothers me,
rasping breaths rolling in and out
like ocean waves on a windy night,
the steady rhythm almost hypnotic
but not quite enough to
carry me along on its currents.

Sometimes I want to poke him,
wresting him from his rest,
to ask how he can ease into sleep
like a bathtub filled with warm water.

But I just look at the clock
and get up at two in the morning
to fold laundry or pay bills,
or rearrange the kitchen cabinets,

or maybe knit a sweater from the fleece
of the thousand sheep
wandering aimlessly
at the foot of our bed.

The Insomniac's Dream Journal

The pen rests in the yawning mouth
of the notebook on my bedside table.
I long to feed its hungry pages
like a sparrow regurgitating
into the eager mouths of her young.
But morning has come again
like a mailman delivering nothing.
Hatchlings gaze up into an empty sky
screeching in their nest,
"Feed me."

What the Gratitude List Said to the Bucket List

Someday I will drink from the Fountain of Youth
and it will taste like champagne
pouring from diamond studded clouds
to erase the frown lines and the laugh lines
and the unread lines of my aging face,
until I am 21 again and this time
I will know how to be young.

> *"Today, cool clean water poured from the faucet."*

Someday I will ride an elephant in Thailand,
sitting astride his bristled back
my hips undulating with each thunderous step.
And he will lift his trunk and blow like Dizzy Gillespie
heralding my arrival at the outskirts of Bangkok
where he will wrap his trunk around my waist
and lower me gently to the ground.

> *"Today, our dog greeted me like Argus when I came home
> from work."*

Someday I will learn to speak French
and stroll the Orangerie at Versailles
*Et je vais l'odeur d'orange fleurs
qui fleurissent dans les jardins*
and men whose lips drip Baudelaire
will perfume me with orange blossoms
and scatter the petals *à mes pieds.*

> *"Today, my husband brought me French Roast coffee in bed."*

Someday I will dine at a five-star restaurant
where a tuxedoed waiter will pull out my chair and
lay a linen napkin in my lap and call me Madame
and the shaved truffles will taste like a rare delicacy
instead of the sweaty socks they actually smell like,
and I will savor them knowingly
as candle light flickers through crystal goblets.

"Today I had enough to eat."

Mass of Remembrance

He pours a glass of wine,
not the Communion wine
reserved for tomorrow morning,
just a stale Merlot
left over from dinner
one night last week.

Nothing sacred,
but helpful perhaps,
as he stares again at the page,
empty but for a few words
scribbled at the top.
Homily—
Sunday, September 16, 2001

He knows
they will come in droves
tomorrow morning,
looking for answers
he does not have.
No chapter or verse
to salve this wound.

"Blessed are the meek?"
They will rise as one
and angrily exit the pews.
"Turn the other cheek?"
Both cheeks are already
swollen and red with tears
of rage and grief.

He wants to nourish their souls
but all the loaves
and all the fishes combined
would not be enough
to feed their hunger
for answers.

51

Neither the Prodigal Son
nor his stodgy brother
have any insights to share.
And Job just shakes his head
in mute resignation.

Another sip of wine,
no after-taste of blood.
For that he turns to the 6:00 News
and listens to the reporters
recounting the death toll.

He drains the last few drops,
stares at the blank page,
and writes the only words
he can muster.

"Let us pray."

Love Letter to Tomorrow

There you are
in tomorrow.
Saturday morning
snorkeling in Da Nang
where there are now
five-star resorts on the coast
of the South China Sea
and Robert Duvall
would love the smell of
mango juice in the morning.
If you hear
The Flight of the Valkyries,
it's only because someone has
set his Pandora station
to Wagner's greatest hits.

While here,
it is still Friday,
and Nice is stained
with a mile long swath of blood
where a truck barreled through
the crowds who gathered
to celebrate freedom.

Here where it is still today,
a coup has broken out in Turkey
where you once visited
the Blue Mosque in Istanbul
and Mary's birthplace in Ephesus.
And at this moment,
the newscaster explains
that she simply
doesn't know what is happening.

As I get ready for bed,
I think of you
half a world away,
and I wonder what tomorrow
will bring.
You are already there.
Can you tell me?

Bumper Sticker Theology on Route 690

The traffic jam turns 690 into a parking lot.
The car in front of me brandishes a slogan.
Worry less; pray more.
So now instead of worrying
about the ice cream and frozen peas
melting in the grocery bags,
I need to worry about
whether I am praying enough?

Do I pray for the cars to miraculously
move down the highway?
And while I'm at it, should I pray
for this country we always ask God to bless?
And let's not forget the polar bears
drowning in the warming waters
of the Arctic Circle.

Is that what she means sitting serenely
behind the wheel of her Camry
offering an Our Father or a Hail Mary?
Or is she the type who can just ad lib?
How you doing, God?
Just thought I'd say hello,
nice job on the sunrise this morning.

Is it really that easy to just show up
like that second cousin you never hear from
until he needs something
and then forgets all about you
until the next time?

Worry less; pray more.
Okay…So can you get this traffic moving, Lord?
I need to get back to the home that shelters me,
to put away the food from this earth you've created
where we live and love and sometimes
remember to give you thanks.

Is that a clearing up ahead?
No…Oh well,
I'll get there eventually.
By the way Lord,
thanks again for that sunrise.

Hiking Koko

Koko Head soars
a thousand feet over the glittering waves
of Hanauma Bay.
Vertical climb.
Too much for the aging tourist
who doesn't know any better.
Temperature a blistering 100 degrees.
Empty water bottle drier
than the dusty bed of the crater below.

The collapse is slow, graceful almost,
as I sink to the railroad ties that mark the ascent.
And then it begins.

Ohana, they call it. Family.
The man who gives me his extra bottle of water.
The young girl in fuscia running shorts
massaging my hand to keep the blood flowing.
The college student who tucks his backpack under my head
while he fans my face with his baseball cap.
The German tourist who hoists my feet over her shoulders,
"To keep your blood circulating," she explains.

I surrender to them all
as they minister to the stranger
lying prostrate on the trail.
Thank you, I say, Mahalo,
a mumbled mantra
uttered down a long corridor
where I hear my own echo.

They shush me as if I were a toddler
struggling against nap-time.
But they need to know what I see
gazing up from my place on the ground
where I witness the tender gestures
of anonymous angels
saving the life of a woman
whose name they will never know.

Rescue at Koko Crater

He descended like a spider from a slender thread.
The chopper blades whirred above the trail.
"Don't be afraid," said his partner.
From the top of the volcano, I could see
a crowd in the parking lot below.

"Don't be afraid," they said,
snapping me into a canvas harness,
"He's the best in the business," said one firefighter.
"I'd let him carry my mother," said his partner.

He hooked my harness to his belt with a steel carabiner.
"Don't be afraid," he said. "We lift cars with these things."
If I could have moved the muscles of my face,
I might have smiled.

He signaled the pilot and we rose in sudden whoosh,
dust and stones swirling in the vortex.
His body was taut as the cable that carried us.
"Don't be afraid," he said.
"Thirty seconds and we'll be back on the ground."

We glided over the turquoise face of Hanauma Bay,
its half-moon coastline fringed with palm trees.
"You might as well open your eyes," he said.
"Tourists can't buy a view like this."
So I looked, and I wasn't afraid.

Paradise Found

So this is Paradise.
Cue the palm trees—
Balmy breezes
bearing the scent
of suntan lotion and plumeria.
Egrets as numerous
as pigeons in Central Park.
A perfect day
darting through waves
where silver-billed dolphins
dance a can-can in the surf.

But my piece of
paradise is sewn
into the seam of light
piercing the clouds
outside our winter-weary
window
spilling a new day
across the rumpled
bedspread
a thousand miles
from the nearest
palm tree.

My own Paradise Found—
not Milton's epic poem
or Waikiki's white sands,
just your face
at the airport
welcoming me home
with a handful of
red carnations.

Emergence

Academia Gallery, Florence

Michelangelo professed to see
the figure deep within the marble.
His job was simply to set it free
from its stone chrysalis.

But not so for St. Matthew
emerging from the block of marble
where the sculptor left him
to fend for himself.

Pulse frozen in the muscled neck,
protruding knee wrenched in agony,
he tries to hurl himself
from the monumental slab.

His eyes blaze
with the effort of emergence,
abandoned before the artist
could set him free,

trapped in a moment
of endless becoming,
his mighty hand repels the stone
to no avail.

The Gardens at Villa Lecchi

The locals are smarter than I am.
They draw the shades and nap
while the sun bakes the stone terrace
overlooking the olive groves.
They will wake later in the day
to the ancient perfume
of roses steeping in the sun—

Roses that still smell like the roses
of a hundred years ago,
Roses mingling with honeysuckle
and sweet basil and lavender,
simmering in the afternoon heat,
Roses in apricot and yellow and crimson,
each hue a voice in a choir
of fragrant variations.

Who can sleep in the midst
of this aromatic concerto,
fragrances singing
on the faintest breeze,
the bees too drunk with it
to care when I lean in,
pressing my cheek to a blossom.

Sweat trickles
between my shoulder blades
and down my back.
The sun burns my neck.
If I had a lick of sense
I'd drift into the parlor
and close my eyes.
But how can sense
outweigh such scents?

At the Gutenberg Museum

"In principio erat verbum."
John 1:1

The replica of Gutenberg's press
is three centuries old.
Oak and bronze.
Taller than me.
A monolith.

The docent asks for a volunteer
and my hand springs up.
She invites me to the platform,
sets a sheet of linen paper in the frame
positions my hands on the wood platen.

"Now…push," she demands,
like a midwife declaring
the time has come for birth.
Obedient, I thrust my body forward.
A grunt rises up from my gut
as my hands feel the weight of words.

She directs me to pull the lever
pressing the type into the paper.
Then we reverse the procedure
and she lifts the plate to reveal the page.

Finally, she delivers it into my hands.
Gospel of John, Chapter One.
Scanning the ornate lettering
for a familiar word,
my high school Latin eludes me.

Amo, amas, amat...
All those lost conjugations
and declensions.
A dead language,
reborn on the page.
Et factum est verbum esset bonum.
And still, the word is good.

Red Carpet

Home from a second tour in Iraq
he stands on the beach
at the Jersey shore—
the rockets' red glare
no longer the prelude
to a baseball game
but the flashpoint
that wakes him from
sweat-drenched nightmares,
where pillars of acrid smoke
stand like sentries
at the borders
of consciousness.

Flashbacks emerge
like black ice
sending him careening
into the darkness—
nothing to do but drive
into the skid
and pray.

He wants to vomit the poison
out of his soul
with a howl that
erupts from his mouth
in ribbons of lava,
unfurling like a burning carpet
spanning the ocean
until it makes landfall
on the Irish coast
and when it reaches that distant shore

he prays for a flock of sea gulls to
snatch it into their beaks
and tear at its fibers until the carpet
falls into the sea
and a school of sharks
ravages the ragged remnants
and the ocean's relentless currents
beat all that's left of it into
a formless mulch
on the ocean floor.

And then,
perhaps,
he will know peace.

Sipping Tea in the Dalai Lama's Chair

Chapel House Retreat Center, Colgate University

I would have expected stanchions and velvet ropes.
Feel free to sit there, the manager says.
A water ring scars the arm
where someone carelessly set their cup.
He would laugh at my trepidation
as I approach the chair made just for him—
wide enough for two but built for one
seated in the lotus position.
Sit, he would say,
as if it were just another chair.

So I bend my knees and slide back
against the red leather cushion.
The chair calls me to stillness,
an invitation to silent surrender,
to gaze through a wall of glass
into autumn woods.
Golden locust leaves
drift slowly to earth
with a languid choreography
that defies gravity.

My tea cup has grown cool in my hands,
the only measure of time
since I climbed into the chair.
I swallow the last tepid sips.
The yellow leaf I have been studying
still holds firmly to its bough.
Rising, I see where my body
has left an impression on the chair,
but not so deep as the impression
the chair has left on me.

The Dry Cleaner's Daughter

For the Rev. Dr. Renee Tembeckjian

In her bedroom above the shop,
she heard the bell jingle
every time the door opened.
His warm voice,
still bearing the accent
of the Armenian refugee,
greeted each customer
with quiet dignity.

She recalls him
as a priest without a collar
presiding over a ritual cleansing—
trusted intermediary
between stain and renewal.

When they slid their garments
across the counter,
he knew their secrets and their longings—
The wine stain on the silk blouse,
the ink on the businessman's cuff,
the smear of paint on the smock.

He made no distinctions among his flock,
tending with equal care
to the season's newest fashions,
and the tired wool coat
that had seen too many winters.

Before the city was awake,
she rose to the early morning clatter
of air compressors rumbling into action,
the hiss of the steam press
perfecting the fine art of the crease,
the screech of hangers scraping

the rod where his practiced fingers
knew exactly where to find
the business suit draped in plastic,
ready for the job interview downtown.

She knew her father
as the custodian of memory
and the steward of dreams
when the bride brought her gown
to be cleaned and boxed,
preserved for the daughter
or granddaughter yet to come.

He was the keeper of secrets
when the Upper East Side lady
brought in her silk unmentionables
and cashmere sweaters
drenched in Chanel No. 5—
knowing he would never ask
who had inhaled the scent
the night before.

While they came and went,
his daughter learned lessons
he never knew he was teaching—
a gospel of dignity and care.
Blue collar or white collar,
every stain could be removed,
every garment restored.

When she became a priest,
she wore her own collar,
clean and starched,
remembering the lessons she learned
from the man who carried her up the stairs

to the apartment over the shop
while she pretended to be asleep.
And every Sunday,
when she climbs the steps
to the pulpit,
she knows he carries her still.

Praise Song for the Hospice Nurse

For Sue Reiffenstein, R.N.

See the rustic cottage by the lake
where she sat as a girl mourning Uncle Buck
while deer and rabbits and turtles
lingered near the water's edge to pay their respects.
Don't try to tell her it was a coincidence.
Even then she knew what grief looked like.

Sit with her at the bedside of ancient relatives
when she was a child in Brooklyn,
Irish brogues murmuring the rosary
while she held a glass of cool water
to great-aunt Maureen's pale lips.

Walk the halls of the hospital
where she learned to ignore the insults
of doctors who would go to any lengths
to keep a body breathing
without ever asking,
What do you want?

See how she learned to wear their slurs
like a superhero's cape—
Angel of Death.
She'll kill your mother.
She's that hospice nurse.

Hear the song she heard
in the rhythm of the death rattle,
quiet at first then building
til its crescendo gave way
to the silent song of peace.

At eighty-two, she is still on call—
But now her medicines are stories.
Her healing art is words.
She will tell she is not a poet.
I will tell you she is a poem.

Ten Rings

I can hear you now
telling me I worry too much
as I dial the number for
the fourth time in an hour
instead of simply assuming
your cell phone has gone dead
on the long stretch of highway.

I tell myself you probably
turned off the Interstate
to follow a country road
like the time you
took the exit marked
Chautauqua just because
you liked the name.

I tell myself that's one of the things
I love about you,
as I imagine you pulling over
to watch a red-tailed hawk
circling a meadow.

I tell myself, soon
we will visit Chautauqua together
because I have to believe
you will be home in just a minute
and we will have time
to plan the trip.

I dial the number again.
Ten rings.
No voice mail.
The phone as useless as
two tin cans and
a broken string.

I tell myself
to stop worrying
as I sit in front of the window,
teacup rattling on the saucer
like teeth chattering in an Arctic wind,
imagining this living room
without you living in it.

I tell myself
soon you will pull into the driveway
and tell me about
the red-tailed hawk you followed
deep into the woods to see
what he was hunting.

I will tell you then
that it is rude and inconsiderate
not to call
when you are running three hours late
and, by the way, I don't give a damn
about the red-tailed hawk.

I will tell you then
that I do not appreciate
this dress rehearsal for widowhood
because I am not ready
for the black dress that hangs in my closet
reserved for such occasions.

I punch the numbers into
the useless phone
for the tenth time.
Headlights pull into the driveway.
I run to the door
so happy to be angry in your arms.

Making Music

The scroll saw sings
as his hand guides it tenderly
over thin sheets of cherry
revealing hourglass curves,

like a shapely woman
lying on her side,
ready to respond
to a skillful touch.

The hum of the sander
drifts up to the kitchen
from his workbench
below.

A dulcimer begins to emerge
from the medley of
of woods and wires,
as he crafts a gift
from father to son.

He plays each tool
like a maestro,
carving, sanding,
stroking the wood,

centering the fret board
on the figured face
between the open mouths
of the sound holes.

Tenderly he threads the strings,
adjusts the tuning knobs,
plucks out the first tentative notes,
filling the air
like a newborn's first cry.

"I don't know where he gets it,"
he muses, pondering
his son's musicality,
"Everything he touches
turns to song."

Love in the Aviary

Love poems have fallen out of fashion.
Gone extinct like the passenger pigeons
of a century ago.
Poems must make a statement
like the rooster
crowing to herald the morning,
loud and insistent,
convinced of its own authority
as it scratches and paws the dirt.

But I prefer the matins
of the mourning doves
heralding that very same dawn
with gentle insistence.
They claim no credit
for the rising of the sun.
They simply rejoice in its light.

Perched outside our window
they keep up their
steady stream of clichés,
obedient to their own rhyme and meter.
Mating for life,
they celebrate the mundane miracle
of a happy marriage.

What I Want

I want you to find my favorite dress,
the blue silk with long sleeves
that I always wore on special occasions.
I want you to send it to the cleaners
and then give it away.
Don't even think of dressing
what's left of me in it.

I want all of the spare parts,
corneas and kidneys, liver and heart,
to be transplanted like the bulbs
that need to be thinned out each fall
before winter hardens the earth.

I want you to be kind to strangers,
because with all those organs
making music in other people,
you'll just never know
who might be carrying a piece of me.

I want you to place my ashes
in the tea tin I keep on my kitchen counter,
the one with the picture
of two cardinals in the snow.
Do not buy an urn.
They tend to be ugly
and far too expensive.

I want you to use the money
you would have spent
on the ugly urn
for a plane ticket to Ireland
and find the apple tree in Killarney
where we scattered
Nanny Marge's ashes
when you were eighteen.

I want you to find a nice B&B
near the cemetery at Aghadoe
where our guide led us to the tree,
leaving the entire tour group
to fend for themselves
while he found the perfect spot
to deposit the dearly departed.

I want you to remember
how he stood at a respectful distance
uttering a quiet prayer
while we poured the ashes
around the tree
twenty paces to the right
of John Cronin's headstone.

I want you to find John Cronin's headstone
and pause under the tree
and memorize every detail of the place—
grass rolling down to the water's edge,
weathered Celtic Crosses blanketed with moss,
watery light piercing the clouds
over the islands dotting the lake.

That's what I want…

But if all that seems a bit too elaborate,
just find a lovely tree and
pour out all that's left.
That's what I really want after all,
to be poured out,
to nourish the soil,
to let nothing go to waste.

The Green Room

With thanks to William Carlos Williams

so much depends
upon

a green paint
swatch

taped to the
wall

against the white
windowsill.

It was meant to be that quick
bright sliver of
summer

light shimmering through the underside of
maple leaves in
June.

But after the walls had dried and
the furniture was back in
place,

the fluorescent green room vibrated as if
we had plunged our paintbrushes into
tubs

of neon lime ice cream and
let it melt down the walls of the
bedroom.

So, in one of those lemonade
out of lemons (or limes)
moments,

we mixed the leftover paint with a
bucket of white and started
again.

Retriever

The dog is a parachute about to open,
gazing at the leash as if willing it into action.

His tail thumps an eager rhythm on the floor
like a jump rope slapping the sidewalk.

Wet grass calls through the open window.
Time to chase the moon out of the sky.

He sees the scent of deer rising
in ribbons of color only a dog's nose can hear.

Poised to chew the dawn like an old sock,
he is patient as a waterfall.

The speeding Porsche of morning beckons,
but she just pats his head.

The coffee cup yawns in her hand.
She yawns in her chair.

Morning yawns outside the window.
His tail taps out a frantic Morse Code.

Ginger Teaches Me How to Die

You'll know what to do when she has more bad days than good.

When I have to carry her
up the two steps onto the porch
and feel her flinch
as I set her down on the floor,
I know this is the worst of the bad days.
She inches her way to the door,
front legs pulling hindquarters
which no longer bend to her will.

Ginger studies me with eyes
that have always reminded me
of Milk Duds melting in the sun.
Her gaze might be saying,
"Today is a good day to die,"
like the Kiowa Dog Soldiers
facing the inevitable with a courage
I can't claim to understand.

She stands still as I wipe the trickle
of blood and pee from her hind legs,
remembering the promise I made years ago
when she dive-bombed the tray
of chocolate fudge brownies
and her torqued belly echoed
under the veterinarian's skillful thump.

Okay, I told her then,
if you live through this,
I promise to give you chocolate
when the time comes.

I dial the vet and peel open
the package of Reese's Peanut Butter Cups.
She watches every move I make
and lies down to savor the feast.

The Prodigal's Sister

She was folding laundry when it happened.
Didn't know what the ruckus was all about
when she saw her father drop to his knees
with his hands raised in the air.
She couldn't tell if it was a stroke
or if the barn was on fire,
or if the farm had been besieged by robbers.
She was betting on the stroke when she heard him
calling out her kid brother's name,
but then he started praising God
and shouting orders to the servants,
and when she looked far across the field,
she saw the skinny shell of the boy-now-man
she had taught herself to forget.

"This does not bode well," she murmured,
scanning the horizon for her older brother
who was out bringing in the sheaves as usual.
He had a laundry list of grievances these days,
against the boy, their father, the world in general,
as if he were the only one who ever lifted a finger.
She could have grumbled too,
but her laundry list was sorted
by darks, lights and delicates,
and she had no time for grudges.

The kid was stumbling now,
and the father, forgetting his own infirmities
hobbled across the field,
lifted him up off the ground,
and threw his finest robe over the boy's shoulders.
She could just imagine how filthy it would be
by the time it found its way into the laundry basket.
But the old man looked happy,
and there were plenty more robes where that came from.

Truth be told, she had missed the kid too.
Anyway, she had a fatted calf to roast,
and those sheets and towels
weren't going to fold themselves.

Martha and the Prodigal's Brother

My sister told me not to get here early.
Don't seem too eager, she said.
Who's eager?
I just want to get it over with.
I've got a house to clean,
and dinner to cook when I get home.
Who has time for all this fuss?

> When my brother said
> he wanted me to meet a woman,
> I almost choked on my cornflakes.
> Back home less than a month
> and he's trying to tell me what to do with my life.
> Besides, I know all about his kind of women.
> But then he said it was Lazarus and Mary's sister.
> I've heard good things about her.
> So I figured I had nothing to lose.

She told me not to wear my hair up.
Let it flow, she said, like water rippling
over your shoulders.
She should talk. Her and that hair.
The scandal of the neighborhood, if you ask me.
No thank you, little sister.
He'll take me as I am or not at all.
So a bun it is. Clean and tidy.
Like a well-kept house.

> He told me I smell like a stable.
> Would a little scented oil kill you? he asked.
> If she can't take the smell of me now, I said,
> she'll never get used to it.
> But I washed my hair and scrubbed the dirt
> from under my finger nails.
> A little dirt never killed a working man, I told him.
> "You should try it some time."

I think I see him standing at the counter,
Yes, the waiter is pointing this way.
He's taller than I thought, clean shaven,
And his hair...see how it shines in the sunlight.
He sees me. Yes, that's him.
He just waved.
Oh Mary, what have you gotten me in to?

>So that's her, in the starched dress,
>a bit younger than I imagined,
>and is she blushing?
>Why does she hide her hands
>under the table?
>I know she saw me.
>Why does she look away?
>Am I really the hulking monster I imagine?

He's walking this way.
Is that a smile?
I wish I had let her polish my nails
like she wanted to.
My knuckles are so cracked and red.
Working hands.
But capable of tenderness, I'm sure.
I suppose I should rise to greet him.

>"No, don't get up."
>I reach out my hand to shake hers.
>I wonder if it will frighten her,
>gnarled and heavy as it is,
>like a lion's paw, like a field hand.
>She takes it haltingly.
>Is that a smile? Yes, it is.

His hand feels strong.
A hand that knows the weight of honest work.
"It's very nice to meet you," I say,
my voice so quiet I can barely hear myself.
Surveying his features fleetingly
I am drawn to the eyes,
brown and dark as the earth
he tends on his father's farm.

                    "And a pleasure to meet you."
                    See how she sits up so straight.
                    I like a woman with good posture.
                    She's the type I could bring home
                    for Sunday dinner.
                    And maybe this time, Dad would finally
                    roast the fatted calf for *me*.
                    "May I get you a cup of coffee?"

"Yes, thank you. Cream, no sugar, please."
When was the last time someone served me?
I think of Mary telling me to lighten up.
"Just be in the moment," she said,
so when I notice the fleck of lint on his shirt,
I take a deep breath and resist the urge
to flick it off, tidy him up.
There will be time for such adjustments—
if need be.
Besides, a little piece of lint never hurt anybody.

The Prodigal Son's Father Attends His First
Al-Anon Meeting

In the church basement
where he has no last name
he sits in a folding chair
under a wall clock
that ticks too loudly.

A half-eaten donut in his hand,
a blank stare in his eyes,
he doesn't weep anymore.
He has nothing left to cry for—
not even the greasy
bones of the fatted calf.

After the homecoming,
his son hocked the ring and the robes
for a case of Thunderbird
and ran off again,
this time taking his brother with him.

Dead sheep,
starved and neglected,
litter his field.
No one to blame but himself.
Still he wishes he could
change the things
he cannot change.

The Zen of Nap Time

For Brayden

Chop wood; carry water,
said the Zen masters of old.
In other words, do what needs doing,
when it needs to be done,
like the baby who cries at midday
to declare the time has come
for nourishment and a nap.

Chop wood; carry water,
Like the mother who hears the cry
and warms the bottle,
testing the temperature
on the back of her wrist,
then feeds him what he needs,
and carries him back to his crib.

Chop wood; carry water,
Like the mother and child,
waiting for sleep to descend,
certain that when the time comes,
each will awaken refreshed
and ready to begin
again.

Cloud Watching with Daniel

Before he learns to read a book,
he reads the sky,
discovering wondrous creatures
in an airborne kaleidoscope
of endlessly shifting light.

At sunset the clouds blush
against the deepening blue
and he points over my left shoulder
commanding me to see
the pink whale propelling slowly
across the horizon.

Had Ahab seen this leviathan,
perfect in size and scale,
he would have abandoned his quest
for the great white
and hurled his harpoon
at the firmament.

Sometimes when Daniel points up,
ecstatic at some new discovery,
I can't quite find
the three-legged dog
or the fire engine racing
through the ether.

But it doesn't matter what I see
etched on the infinite blue canvas.
It's what I see in the infinite blue eyes
of the three-year-old holding my hand
that reminds me
anything is possible.

Souvenir

The music it hears is the echo of
fingers tapping threads into fabric.
Warp weft, tap tap warp weft.
A picture slowly emerging.
Tap tap tapping with the comb
Hand carved for just this purpose.
The loom, like a harp, strung precisely,
sounds each note.
Nimble brown fingers stained with dye
ply their craft instinctively,
green darker than the pine forests that skirt the town,
red deeper than the New Mexico sunset.
A landscape measuring three feet wide, five feet long,
spreads before the couch in my office.

It pretends to be a rug,
but in fact it is the receptacle of desert rain,
still bearing the distant scent of the open air market
across the street from the Georgia O'Keeffe Museum
where well-dressed tourists
finger the cool turquoise beads and clay pots
they will carefully pack into their luggage,
and I bought a rug for my office floor
where it still listens for the song of the loom
and the comb tapping down
strands of wind and sun
and the soft chatter of the Pueblo women
selling their wares.

The Day Before Doomsday...Again

And what if it's true this time?
What if tomorrow really is the day
when the Book of Revelations
and the Mayan Calendar collide?

What if the madmen have their way?
Count to three, push the button?
What if a rogue nation
or a stray asteroid finally
obliterates our hemorrhaging planet?

What time will it happen?
Morning? Afternoon?
Will I have time enough
for one more walk in the woods?
Time to watch sunlight
permeate the silver filaments of a spider web
trembling on a birch branch?
Time enough to see the New England asters
lift their faces to the golden locust leaves?

And what if the prophets of doom
are wrong again
and Sunday comes around
as it likely will?
Will I remember the woods are still there
like a beloved grandmother I should visit more often?
Will I gaze upon the veins
of a red maple leaf
as if I were studying a map
to lead me home?

Snowy Egret—Avery Island, Louisiana

Luminous apparition
teetering on the shoreline,
framed by Spanish moss
in molten Southern air,
balancing on blade thin legs—
a runway model with her high heel
stuck in the mud.

Hailing from the land
of dusky pigeons
with city sooted wings,
I reach for my camera,
sweat beading down my back
as I line up the image,
centering her in a perfect balance
between river and sky.

"If you must,"
the regal bird seems to say,
bending her graceful neck
to coyly tuck her beak
under one wing
and winking at me with
one jet black eye
years before any of us
had ever heard of the
Deepwater Horizon
or tried to count its costs.

The Wild Boars of Fukushima

They wander in packs
through the ancestral home of
Godzilla and Rodan—
no, not the sculptor...
the mutant pterodactyl
who screeched through
Japanese movie theaters
less than a decade after
the bomb unleashed
its flood of monstrosities.

They stroll down deserted streets,
set up housekeeping
in the abandoned homes
of villagers who fled
first the earthquake
and its attendant tsunami,
and then the meltdown at
the world's largest
nuclear power plant.

Gorging on poisoned grasses,
swilling contaminated water,
and still they thrive—
over 13,000 at last count.
Too aggressive to domesticate.
Too radioactive to eat.
Too resilient to die.

Officials say the villagers
cannot return
because the wild boars
pose such a threat to public safety.
Well that's a relief.

At least it's not
radioactive fall-out
from the meltdown.
Glad to know it's simply
an invasion of wild boars—
just like the ones in Chernobyl.

Celtic Wind

Lingering between goodbye and goodnight,
you shudder under my gaze,
grey and icy,
like the wind that heralds an Irish dawn
and sweeps sleepy fishermen into morning,
leaving thatched roofs
and wood-burning stoves
and women crying on the doorstep
fearing the hour
when only promises will return on the waves,
and an empty boat in pieces
on the rocky western shore.

Having mastered the art of the goodbye kiss,
we stand uncertainly in the doorway.
your voice see-saws between memory and tomorrow
and our hands dangle awkwardly at our sides.
Aware of our inability to make small talk
we stare, never touching,
hoping to retrieve a tattered oath,
a promise to part friends.
Suddenly alone,
I watch you row out to sea,
bracing myself against the chill.

Watching Billy Collins Read His Poems

He stands center stage,
a spotlight beaming
down on his perfectly polished
hairless dome, tufts of fringe
poking out at the sides as if he had
just run his fingers through it in search
of the perfect noun that would speak for itself
without leaning on a needless adjective,
like needless, for example.

The eyes, always at work, evoke
another poet from centuries past
who bore the same surname and
fringed oval pate,
whose close-set eyes
could see the tragedy
lurking in the margins
of every comedy
and vice-versa.

Reading glasses perched on his nose
delivering his lines matter-of-factly
with an ever present half smile,
(but only half),
I imagine him in Elizabethan collar and
knobby-kneed green tights
and wonder if they might be distant cousins.

Just imagine what might have been
if the Bard's mother had said,
"What's in a name?"
and called her William, Billy.
Perhaps he would have compared his lover to
a bowl of Cheerios
instead of a summer's day.

Hamlet, poor lad,
might have chosen simply to be.
And Cordelia could have given her father
a bowl of perfectly ripened pears
and gone back to France.

Breakfast Bearing the Name of the Poet Into Heaven

> *"He's gone."*
> —*"Fergus Falling"*

We ate oatmeal that morning
as a tribute to the poet who conjured Keats
to his table to ruminate on the
gloppy texture of the toothless concoction.

Instead of the blue-tinged skim milk he reviled,
I simmered ours in apple cider.
We ate it together because, as the poet said,
It is not good to eat oatmeal alone.

His obituary sat open on the kitchen table,
like a guest come to share the meal
that might have been more to his liking
topped with his beloved blackberries.

The headline read, *"Galway Kinnell
Plain-Spoken Poet, Is Dead at 87."*
A photo showed him at an old typewriter
hammering away at the letters
like shingles on a barn roof.

After breakfast we washed the dishes
and drank our second cup of coffee,
reading his poems to each other,
as if they were hymns.

Dear Mary Oliver,

Thank you for inviting me to eavesdrop
on your conversations with the grasshopper;
for allowing me to follow at a safe distance
during your solitary walks through the fields
just beyond your back door.

Thank you for transforming the shoulder
of the road into an altar
when I see the body of a dead
deer or black snake lying there;
and for urging me to pause
and bow my head like a mourner
filing past the coffin of a fallen president.

Thank you for teaching me that the
gradual decline of aging eyesight
is simply a command to look more closely,
study more deeply, see with my heart.

Thank you for instructing me in the arts of
reverence and presence and gratitude.
You who say you don't know
"exactly what a prayer is,"
are the author of my morning vespers,
and the psalmist whose voice I hear
in the honking of the wild geese.

Waiting for the Tulips to Bloom

Glass bud vases
line the kitchen windowsill,
empty but for the light
pouring through them,
waiting impatiently
for the tulips to bloom,
scarlet and fuchsia
amethyst and magenta
and yellows for which
there are no names.

They have spent the winter
politely tolerating
supermarket carnations
and alstroemeria
flown in from greenhouses
in Texas and Florida,
parodies of spring
gracing the dining room table.

Light shimmering
through the cut glass
dapples the kitchen floor,
on this sunny day
when the welcome rays
cannot compete
with the frigid breath
of an April grown weary
of its legendary cruelty.

And still they wait,
longing to hold stems
still moist with dew,
petals dusty with pollen
sticky with the bee's
early morning
dalliances.

Submission

Attached please find five poems that are no less
than the sum total of my self-worth.
Please know that if you do not deign to publish them,
you will confirm every self-doubt
that has plagued me since junior high,
reducing me once again to the zit-dotted, chubby girl
who believed the horrible things her classmates
whispered behind her back in gym class.

Faced with the resounding thud of your rejection,
I will know that in the great used car lot of poetry,
I am indeed the 1973 powder blue Ford Pinto
with dented fender and cracked windshield.

Plunging into despair,
I will, once again, seek solace in the bottom
of a box of Oreos, which, I suppose
is better than a bottle of bourbon,
unless you happen to be Ernest Hemingway,
who quite frankly would have looked ridiculous
scarfing down cookies and milk
on the beach in Key West.

But I digress…
Attached, please find five poems
for your consideration.
They are stained with my very life's blood—
which is only a cliché if it's not true,
so I leave the decision entirely in your hands.
No pressure.

Wisdom Quilt

I believe "we convince by our presence."[1]
I believe "a foolish consistency *is* the hobgoblin of little minds,"[2]
And "it's not what you look at that matters, it's what you see,"[3]
I believe "the future lies in the hands of the creatively maladjusted[4]
And that "faith is taking the first step even when you cannot see
   the whole staircase."[5]
I believe that "Hope is the thing with feathers/That perches
   in the soul,"[6]
And I believe "All you need is love."[7]
I believe "you've got to wake up every morning with a smile
   on your face,
And show the world all the love in your heart."[8]
And I believe, "We shall never know all the good that a simple
   smile can do."[9]
I believe in "The peace of wild things,"[10]
And that "happiness really is a warm puppy."[11]
I believe in the "poems and prayers and promises,"[12]

---

[1] Walt Whitman

[2] Ralph Waldo Emerson

[3] Henry David Thoreau

[4] Martin Luther King, Jr.

[5] Martin Luther King, Jr.

[6] Emily Dickinson

[7] John Lennon

[8] Carole King

[9] Mother Teresa

[10] Wendell Berry

[11] Charles Schulz

[12] John Denver

Of those who have gone before me.
I believe "All sorrows can be borne if you can put them into
a story,"[13]
And "there is no greater agony than bearing an untold story
inside you."[14]
I believe in stitching together the fabric of other people's wisdom
and wrapping myself in the quilt of their insights to find out
who I am.
I believe I am the offspring of Walt Whitman and Maya Angelou,
Ralph Waldo Emerson, Isak Dinesen, and John Denver,
Martin Luther King Jr., Carole King, Wendell Berry, the Beatles,
Emily Dickinson, Stephen Sondheim, Snoopy, Mother Teresa,
and my own mother who said,
"Go write a story."[15]

---

[13] Isak Dinesen

[14] Maya Angelou

[15] Margaret Cahill

Afterword

Gloria's Gratitude List

If gratitude is at the heart of this book, then it is the people in my life who are at the heart of that gratitude. So it is with a grateful and humble heart that I thank everyone who helped with this collection:

My teachers and colleagues at Le Moyne College, especially Linda Pennisi, Patrick Lawler and David Lloyd;

Raymond Hammond and New York Quarterly Books for their commitment to this book;

Leah Maines and her team at Finishing Line Press who published my chapbook, *Some of Our Parts*;

Deidre Neilen and the wonderfully supportive community she has fostered at SUNY Upstate Medical Center's *Healing Muse*;

My dear friends in the Poetry as a Spiritual Practice Workshop which I have the great joy of leading at Trinity Episcopal Church in Fayetteville, NY who have shepherded many of these poems through numerous drafts: Laura Bufano CSJ, Judy Carr, Sue Cenci, Sue Gibson, Marie Jerge, Alice Irwin, Susanne Merchant, and Sylvia O'Connor;

Phil Memmer, Georgia Popoff and everyone at the Syracuse YMCA's Downtown Writers Center;

Dan Roche for his brilliant cover photo, and Rachel Ablan who designed the cover;

The beloved friends and family members who have inspired and encouraged so many of these poems, especially Margaret and Edward Cahill, Alicia Cahill Goldberg, Eddie and Vickie

Cahill, Shannon, Dan, Daniel and Brayden Beers, the whole host of Heffernans: Cam, Tra Pham, Maxwell, Maddox, Aaron, Beth, Seamus, William, Anna, Jimmy, Emily, Lila and Jude Saarinen, Barbara Coates, Sheri Goldhirsch, Helen Churko, Walter Levy and Renee Tembeckjian.

And most of all, my beloved husband, first reader and best friend, James M. Heffernan who taught me that half a century is not too long to wait for an *anam cara*.

With gratitude to and for you all.

CPSIA information can be obtained
at www.ICGtesting.com
Printed in the USA
FSHW011613161220
76783FS